Susan Saint Sing

Living *with* Sickness

a struggle toward meaning

Nihil Obstat: Rev. Andre McGrath, O.F.M.
Rev. John J. Jennings

Imprimi Potest: Rev. Jeremy Harrington, O.F.M.
Provincial

Imprimatur: +James H. Garland, V.G.
Archdiocese of Cincinnati
May 20, 1986

The *nihil obstat* and *imprimatur* are a declaration that a book or pamphlet is considered to be free from doctrinal or moral error. It is not implied that those who have granted the *nihil obstat* and *imprimatur* agree with the contents, opinions or statements expressed.

"It's possible" (#22, p. 55) from A Book for the Hours of Prayer in *Selected Poems of Rainer Maria Rilke*, A Translation From the German by Robert Bly. Copyright ©1981 by Robert Bly. Reprinted by permission of Harper & Row, Publishers, Inc.

Book and cover design by Robert Roose

SBN 0-86716-099-3

©1987, Susan Saint Sing
All rights reserved
Published by St. Anthony Messenger Press
Printed in the U.S.A.

It's possible I am pushing through solid rock
in flintlike layers, as the ore lies, alone;
I am such a long way in I see no way through,
and no space: everything is close to my face,
and everything close to my face is stone.

I don't have much knowledge yet in grief—
so this massive darkness makes me small.
You be the master: make yourself fierce, break in:
then your great transforming will happen to me,
and my great grief cry will happen to you.

—Rainer Maria Rilke

Foreword

I hesitate to begin this book. My fear is that you will think that I have something good and beautiful to say about sickness and disability. Worse, you may feel that, because I have written, my story is somehow special, unique.

I have found little good in sickness or in pain. I have suffered, but my story is far less spectacular and much less serious than many others'—perhaps than yours. So please do not look for answers in this book. Sometimes questions are the best I can do. But perhaps the questions themselves are answer enough in that, with them, you and I begin the pursuit of One who is already the pursuer.

I intend to recount the struggle as I experienced it: first bodily, then emotionally and, finally, spiritually. This journey is not solely a look into myself, however, but rather an account of how I have learned, through my sickness, to understand the stories of others. In relating these stories to you, my hope is that you too will find your place among them.

I borrow heavily from the works, thoughts and sufferings of several great men and women. In doing so, I acknowledge their greater talent and attempt to extend the range and deepen the meaning of my own words. More, in drawing upon the experience of all kinds of people—authors and readers, doctors and patients, men and women, children and adults, rich and poor—I attempt to focus on one universal truth: Sickness and pain diminish us all, so we all must strive to diminish them.

If I could copy and thereby call my own the whole of C.S. Lewis's preface to *The Problem of Pain*, I would. It is one of the finest spiritual apologias I've ever read. Since I cannot claim his words, I will try to reiterate his position—adding that I am the fool he is not: "For the far higher task of teaching fortitude and patience I was never fool enough to suppose myself qualified, nor have I anything to offer my readers except my conviction that when pain is to be borne, a little courage helps more than much knowledge, a little human sympathy more than much courage, and the least tincture of the love of God more than all."

In memory of my Dad

Contents

1. Facing Disaster   1
2. Getting Worse   7
3. Seeking Help   13
4. Reclaiming Life   19
5. Coping With the Simple Things   25
6. Admitting Fear   31
7. Reaching Out for Support   39
8. Working Through the Stages   45
9. Facing Mortality   49
10. Discovering Our Creaturehood   55
11. Understanding God's Will   59
12. Praying for Healing   65
13. Overcoming Evil   71
14. Finding Meaning in Sickness   77
Afterword   83
For Further Reading   84
Acknowledgments   85

1

Facing Disaster

We have all witnessed illness or injury. As human beings we naturally tend to believe these things will happen to someone else, not us. This book is about what happens and what can happen when *we* are the stricken ones, when suffering touches *our* family, *our* selves, *our* friends. It deals not only with the physical side of illness but also with the circumstances that complicate recovery and the ability to right our world and our hope again.

Coping with illness or injury is easy in the short run: a broken arm, flu, appendicitis, sprains. We usually recover quickly from these. At times they can even be used as social ploys: There's a certain glamor in sitting around the ski lodge with a cast on your leg.

But when you are faced with a serious, long-term condition, it's a whole different ball game. It is difficult to distract yourself for a lifetime, no matter how strong you think you may be. The challenges that rock your faith, your patience, your life—you don't cut these off and throw them away in four to six weeks as you do a cast. The ramifications of a long-term disease or injury are much farther reaching.

I had years of endurance training for long-distance running. I "toughed out" both acute and chronic injuries, plodded through downpours over soggy cross-country courses, ran up and down hills in wavy summer heat, skied in subzero weather, played basketball on a sprained ankle. I once ran a marathon, passed out a quarter of a mile from the finish, came to, got back up and ran to finish in third place. In college I pulled my hamstring coming out of the blocks in the 100-yard dash. It dropped me face-first onto a cinder track. Yet I could almost always focus myself away from the pain or the extent of my injury. I knew they would be short-lived no matter how much they hurt at the time.

In some ways, I guess, I saw myself immune to any serious injury. A sense of invincibility stems from being young, in good shape and physically active. The personal reality of daily pain or disability was unimaginable to me, but I was soon to find it out.

The university chapel was still and close. Rain clung to the frosted opaque windows. No lights were on. My wet Adidas sneakers made squeaking sounds on the flagstone floor till I reached the carpet and knelt down in a pew. It was the beginning of Lent, 1974.

The large ecumenical chapel showed no signs of Lenten purples. A great brass cross sat on the stone altar, backdropped by a 1960's collage of fabric and wood. I was alone except for the rain, the stillness and this cross.

Earlier that morning I had received a call from home telling me that my father, who had suffered a stroke two years before, was now experiencing coronary complications requiring surgery, a very dangerous proposal in his already deteriorated condition. The doctors wanted to increase the blood flow from his legs to his heart and chest—a flow restricted by arteriosclerosis. All this was further complicated by his diabetes.

I had never before gone into a church to pray. I had gone to Mass diligently for years, but that was because Catholics *had* to go. Given a choice, I would have been off skiing, hiking, boating or doing a myriad of other more interesting things. I had never really prayed for anything in my whole life, yet here I was begging God to make my father well, to let him live.

I must have appeared intensely distraught. A priest who had come in entered my pew and sat next to me without my even being aware of his presence. When I had finished praying, I opened my eyes and there he was, praying too. I didn't know how long he had been there.

He said he had never seen me around before. I said I was new. He invited me to join him and a group of students who would be meeting later that evening for what he called a "charismatic prayer meeting." He said they would all pray for my dad.

I went to the meeting that night. I tried to be congenial. It had been a gracious invitation. I wanted to pray for my dad, but I wanted no part of some fanatical group. I didn't really believe in God, especially in a God who actually wanted to help me. My prayer in the chapel was more an attempt to play it safe, to cover all the bases, just in case. That evening I carried my skepticism like a shield.

Sitting down, I quickly surveyed the group. I had preconceived notions of eye-glassed, straight-laced students reading leather-jacketed Bibles, guys wearing white shirts and girls all in skirts. I was wrong. For the most part, these kids looked just like me: rows and rows of students in sneakers and jeans with backpacks full of books. They sat in concentric circles with eyes raised, palms open and voices singing. Their joy was evident; they loved what they believed.

Baffled and confused, I left. It seemed frightening to me that all this God-stuff might be true. The scene in that room haunted me, though, and the next day I contacted their priest. I learned that this was just one of thousands of such groups across the United States and the world which were part of the charismatic movement.

This group became the central focus of my life for the next four years. The prayer group pulsed with love warmth and understanding; we enjoyed life and one another. This was a terrific time for me, an experience which literally changed my perspective on life 180 degrees. Had I not known such authentic people, I doubt I would ever have thought a personal relationship with God was possible.

A "personal relationship with God" never meant much to me. I actually resented hearing people talk about something I considered so pious and dramatic. I know now it isn't pious or dramatic at all. A personal relationship with God begins whenever we realize he really *is*. From that moment on, nothing can ever be the same. Perhaps other people grow up with this knowledge, or grasp it sooner than I did. But for me it was total gift, delight, almost ecstatic joy.

It was in the midst of this spiritual epiphany that I was abruptly faced with two great traumas. In January 1976 my father died. My world teetered but I tried to hold on to my belief that God knew what he was doing. Less than three months later, I was accidentally dropped on my head during a volleyball exercise.

In the exercise, I would do a handstand against my partner's heels and place my feet over her shoulders. She would then pull me off the ground, back-to-back, in order to stretch my spine. After I was stretched out, she would lower me to the floor so we could reverse positions and do her spine. But my partner accidentally let go of my ankles and I came crashing down, headfirst, onto a carpet-covered concrete floor. As a varsity athlete, I was accustomed to sports-related injuries. So when I felt no pain, I knew I was seriously hurt.

Several doctors examined me, each passing me on to someone else. Opinions included a possible broken neck, a broken back, a herniated disc, bruised nerve roots—or any combination of the four. If the diagnoses were confusing, the initial treatments were even more so. I was set up in traction by one doctor and taken out of it by another. I was iced down and heated up and finally told to go home and come back later in the week when an orthopedic surgeon, who was coming to look at the football players' injuries, would read my X-rays to be sure no vertebrae were broken.

He read them. I was "relatively fine," he said. I

should expect to regain the ability to turn my neck and to use my right arm as soon as the swelling subsided. As I held the white prescription slips for physical therapy, a cervical collar, painkillers, muscle relaxants and anti-inflammatory drugs in my hand, I wondered what exactly "relatively fine" meant.

The feeling of jelly in my neck and back slowly turned into a hot, raging pain. Any flexion of my back felt as if someone had slid a hot, sharp blade through the vertebrae of my upper spine. I could not sit or lie down without assistance. I clearly remember my roommates helping me in and out of bed, into chairs, cars, etc. I took all my final exams while standing propped against the classroom walls, writing in my exam booklet.

I was asked to give the benediction at the women's all-sports banquet. Everyone smiled when, standing stiff in my cervical collar, I grinned impishly and asked them to thank God for our successful season and the health of our athletes.

2

Getting Worse

Several months passed. Feeling a little better, I decided to spend my summer vacation as planned: working in a retreat house in Assisi, Italy.

I needed a restful place that would allow me time and space to recuperate and think. Not only was I still working through the death of my father, but I was acutely aware that my future in physical education might now be limited. My second major, liberal arts, had been for my pleasure, my enrichment. I now had to decide whether I could make some sort of a living at it after graduation.

Assisi, the home of St. Francis, seemed like the perfect place for the summer. St. Francis was a saint I identified strongly with. Animals, nature, all the moods of weather and creation were like a mirror into which Francis looked and found God's reflection. Perhaps the medieval tenor of his legends intrigued me, drawing me back into my own childhood fantasies of great kings, courtly love, knighthood and chivalry. No doubt I identified with the glory of it all, not the day-by-day hardship of abject poverty, brutal warfare, disease and oppression. I wanted only to be near where Francis had lived, to see his city and walk through his forests, hoping a part of him was still there. With $100 in my pocket for the three-month stay, an open plane ticket, and a fearless (albeit naive) enthusiasm, I was off.

Upon landing in Luxembourg I embarked on a 24-hour train ride to Italy. After an electrical storm in the Alps caused the train to lose power and run backwards down the track, and after I missed all my prearranged connections to Assisi and spent hours waiting alone on train platforms, I wondered why I had ever talked myself into this at all. But when the train finally pulled into the Assisi station and I looked up toward the mountain at the red-tiled roofs and towers behind Assisi's ancient walls, I knew it would all be worth it.

With the close Umbrian heat settling around my neck, I took off my cervical collar and tossed it into a trash can. As irresponsible as that may sound, no definite diagnosis had ever been reached. Follow-up treatment plans were a hodgepodge of ideas that constantly varied. Interest (the doctors' and mine) in some type of sustained therapy routine had waned rapidly as the acute phase of my injury passed. Everyone felt I was sufficiently recovered to return to normal daily activity, wearing the collar in crowds and cars to avoid reinjury. But in the 90-degree heat of the Umbrian plain, it seemed more a burden than a blessing.

As an athlete, I was used to a work-it-through attitude. I started my chores of dishwashing, changing bed linens and serving meals for up to 50 people without noticing any substantial discomfort or disability. The chance to work those muscles a bit suited me fine, for I had spent months being anxious about every little move.

I went through my daily routine in the *pensione*, barely noticing the subtle alterations I was making to favor my right arm. But in the evenings after work, when I took my daily walk up to the medieval fortress of the Rocca Maggiore, I began tucking my right hand into my pants pocket because my shoulder ached if I let my arm swing free. I rationalized that my muscles were just weak and tired from working; they would get stronger.

Many of my aches and pains I attributed to the new environment, the stress of meeting people, speaking a different language, the heat, the altitude, etc. It wasn't until I was back at school in the fall that I realized my slight but constant headache could no longer be attributed to traveling.

So began a subtle degeneration of my health, followed by gradual, unconscious decisions to use my arm and shoulder less and less.

Only when I graduated from college a year later and moved to Cincinnati did I become aware that I was replacing almost every movement of my right hand with my left. I grabbed gallons of milk left-handed. I opened and closed car doors left-handed. I carried groceries, laundry, packages—all with my left hand. Even my sleeping position had altered. Normally a stomach sleeper, I switched to sleeping on my back with my head laid to the right, just so, in order to alleviate pain.

I'm not even sure I was aware of how many activities I cut down on or cut out of my life altogether. I found myself glibly declining invitations to go canoeing, hiking, dancing: "No thanks, I don't feel like it." It took quite a while before I realized I was actually saying: "No thanks, I don't *physically* feel like doing much of anything."

I tried my hand at free-lance writing and music composition. Though I published over 30 songs, it was still necessary to supplement my meager artist's income. Dishwasher, roofer, counter clerk, ski sales—I went through a list of jobs that had to be abandoned, one-by-one, as my pain incapacitated me more and more over the next four years.

My last job was driving a school bus for the retarded and handicapped. I had a monitor who loaded the wheelchairs and strapped the children into their seats for me. Still, driving—opening and closing the door, shifting the gears, the long hours of stopping and starting—became an ordeal. By the afternoon pick-up run, I sometimes could barely feel my right shoulder; it grew numb from tightening muscle spasms. Turning in my bus keys, I decided to rest and relax over the summer and not look for work again until the fall.

Summer came and went. With the onset of fall and its burst of autumn colors, I tried to start a daily exercise habit: walking in the afternoon. I lived near the second largest cemetery in the U.S., a beautiful, secluded sanctuary of woods, ponds and streamlets, with countless varieties of birds, plants and small wildlife. If you walked in far enough, it wasn't uncommon to see a red fox stealthily making its way across a ridge or through a ravine. It was the closest thing I had to cherished memories of Pennsylvania woodland. Its beauty distracted me from my daily pain. It became a place I would retreat to often.

The cemetery became a backdrop for me to think about all that had happened in my life. In the face of the frailty bred by my own mortality, the acres of stones became my mentors, listening and, at times, even answering my questions of why, why, why? The paradox of attraction and abhorrence drew me. I walked and searched for answers in the stillness of afternoon's light held briefly in the air or lost silently in the depths of murky water. Death and life abounded there.

I vividly remember one November evening, when all the leaves, long since fallen from the trees, lay dry and brown along the pond's edge. I thought I heard a crackling, rustling sound. "It's just an animal," I tried to reassure my already quickening pulse. Getting more frightened as the sound broadened out across the entire length of the opposite bank, I strained through the dusk to pick out not some creature from beyond the grave, but a flock of 50 to 60 Canada geese walking clumsily down the leaf-laden bank, plopping here and there into the water.

Breathing a sigh of relief, I got up to walk home. I tied my arm snug to my hip with a scarf drawn around my waist—tucking my hand into my pants pocket no longer sufficed. I can still hear myself rationalizing, "It will get better. I am doing better. Pretty soon I'll be *running* over here to see the geese every afternoon."

But eventually I could no longer even take these

walks. The trees, flowers, reflecting ponds, hawks, quiet snows and lazy fish that had mesmerized me through the seasons became faint images of a peace I was losing. My escapes to the cemetery were limited to an occasional car ride through its paths. My contact with the magnificent geese was reduced to hearing them fly away overhead. My world was closing down.

3

Seeking Help

At the beginning, I had thought I could deal with my physical decline. "It can't last forever," I would tell myself. I tried to distract myself, forget about it, concentrate on other things. I'd try to convince myself that it was all just temporary; I could overcome it.

Somewhere in the middle of all this, I even began coping with *some* of my disabilities. I had already begun to pattern a life around my discomfort. But I still kept telling myself, "This amount of sickness I can live with for awhile." In short, I never relinquished my hope that I would be healthy one day soon.

But, eventually, I had to stop kidding myself, let go and fearfully allow myself to know that my sickness was going to be there, maybe for the rest of my life, every hour of every day.

With this realization, my inner world went to

pieces. I stopped going to Mass; I became sullen and somewhat bitter. I was inflexible, irritable and drained. Any effort to accommodate friends or tolerate new situations seemed unbearable. I basically just wanted to be left alone. I didn't want to have to deal with one more thing—not God, not work, not relationships, not anything.

The pain in my neck, back and head was increasing, usually accompanied by migraine headaches, blurred vision and nausea—symptoms which sometimes didn't go away for days. In that time there was no way to read or somehow forget that I hurt. I would lie in bed for hours thinking I was only 28 years old and my life was slipping away. The world became something "out there." My sole preoccupation became a concentrated effort to lie still so I wouldn't hurt.

I had seen every medical expert anyone could think of sending me to. We even started discussing the possibility of the Mayo clinic, except that not one doctor could be pinned down to a solid idea for the referral. An orthopedic surgeon suggested a CAT scan, believing my neck really had been broken in college. This extensive type of X-ray could show where the inner, spinal-cord side of my vertebrae might have been cracked but missed by the traditional X-rays taken in college. He later changed his mind on treating me altogether and referred me to the chief of neurology at a large hospital, who deemed the CAT scan unnecessary. We tried another cervical collar, more tests and another referral to *another* orthopedic surgeon who examined me for all of five minutes and said I had chronic neck strain! Back to the neurologist's where we started drug therapy with a specialized neuromuscular medicine and aspirin. Basically, I had to learn to live with it.

At a loss with the medical world, I turned to chiropractors. I kept the telephone numbers of two chiropractors with me nearly all the time. Initially, they were able to relieve the pain almost completely. I felt more mobile and active after each visit. The only problem was that I practically had to camp next door to their offices because my visits increased from once monthly to twice weekly as their technique, for some reason, effected less and less pain relief.

By February 1983 I had spent two months flat on my back in bed. Unable to flex my back, out of work, in an apartment overrun with roaches and mice, I saw my living space become a shambles. I could do nothing but watch dishes pile up. Food cooked by friends was left half eaten. I simply did not have the physical ability to maintain the basic essentials of life any longer.

Then one morning, through a friend's intervention, I found myself standing outside University Hospital's Pain Control Center. Afraid to go in and afraid not to, I probably would have turned tail and run were it not for a white-coated doctor with his foot in a cast, riding around in an electric cart. He sensed my distress, backed the cart up to the glass entrance and motioned to me, "Come in, come in." My immediate impression was that this man so awkwardly trying to maneuver his cart away from the glass had some firsthand understanding of pain and incapacity. I would talk to him.

After nearly an hour of interview and examination in which he truly listened to my evaluation of past treatments, he withdrew and consulted with his staff. In drastically simplified terms, his diagnosis was that previous treatments had failed because they had neglected to recognize the proper sequence of events. My present muscle spasms and the referred pain accompanying them were not caused by an irritation of the nerve root at the spine. Rather, the atrophied muscles which could no longer sufficiently support my shoulder and scapula were contracting involuntarily, thereby compressing the cervical nerve root and causing the referred pain. So the previous treatments of cervical collars and traction, while effective in the acute phases of my injury to relieve pressure and swelling, were contraindicated in the later stages of my recovery. They served instead to stretch and aggravate the already overworked muscles, causing more pain, more spasm, more muscle fatigue, more nerve compression.

It seemed this cycle had continued over the years because my back muscles never "knew" the injury was over; their protective, reflexive spasming never unlocked. Had I received proper therapy for the massive soft-tissue injury at its onset, I might well have recovered completely years ago.

The doctor suggested a threefold recovery regimen of TENS (transcutaneous electronic nerve stimulator), physical therapy and cervical plexus nerve blocks. He offered no guarantees but hoped for at least a 50-percent decrease in pain.

A TENS unit is a battery-operated device which sends an electrical impulse across the skin between two carefully selected points. The current flowing across the skin interrupts the signal of pain being sent to the spinal cord and on to the brain. So even though the pain exists, its impulse never reaches and registers in the brain and, therefore, no pain is experienced. The stimulus seems to aid in the recovery process, too, by gently toning up the surrounding muscle fiber itself.

Simply stated, a nerve block consists of injecting a long-acting anesthetic around a nerve in order to numb those areas that the nerve passes through. A typical example of a minimal nerve block effect is getting a novacaine shot from the dentist. In my case, a cervical plexus block in my neck numbed the right side of my upper body: shoulder, scapula, right arm, face and back of my head. The muscles that particular nerve signals relax, thereby relieving the spasms. In this state blood and nutrients are free to replenish the muscle fiber with oxygen and carry away cellular wastes which the constricting spasms trapped. The block essentially enables the muscle to recuperate and lets the body heal itself.

All in all, I am one of the lucky ones. After well over 50 such blocks, extensive physical therapy and other care, I am on the tail end of recovering from this injury. I will be able to live a productive life with no lasting paralysis or physical disfiguration, though I will most likely have residual pain and poor health throughout the rest of my life.

Often I have been my own worst enemy. Basically one who detests suffering of any sort, I tended toward the pessimistic end of the spectrum and found it difficult to keep afloat emotionally. It took an all-out effort and the help of friends, therapists and people at the Pain Control Center not only to heal my back but also to heal my whole outlook on life.

For when we find ourselves facing the realization that life is now going to mean coping with something severe, we want to turn our entire self away and pretend it's not so. But for many of us it is so. And it takes courage and concern—our own and others'—not only for the ailing part, but often for our total emotional makeup. For what we do from this realization on shapes the success or failure of living with an illness.

4

Reclaiming Life

As the treatments progressed and my pain decreased a bit, I began to process some of the happenings within me. One of the first things I had to contend with was the feeling that my world was out of control. Nothing seemed to work. My body seemed to fail me in even the simplest things. Then I began to see that, as my own world had entropied—collapsed to an almost lifeless mess—small mental notes began adding up in my mind. Just as my body had gone into a pain cycle where one thing influenced another till outside intervention was required to break the vicious circle, I had also lapsed into a similar negative cycle emotionally and spiritually. I had given up not only hope and faith, but also relationships, creativity, enjoyment, love, etc. These attributes that make life worth living don't disappear when we are sick, but their vitality is so dampened by our own morose feelings that they *seem* to have vanished.

This direct association between body and spirit the ancient Greeks called *arete*. The Greek ideal portrayed the human person as made up of three integral parts—body, mind and soul—whose equilateral forces, if perfected, combined to form one balanced whole. If one was out of kilter, the other two were directly affected. Modern science recognizes the possibility that an ailing soul or mind can cause an affliction of the body. Tension and stress have been known to contribute to heart attacks, strokes and ulcers; some even point to their role in the development of cancer and arthritis, along with a host of other maladies.

In the same way, when physical health deteriorates, mind and soul weaken commensurately. Neuropsychiatry is just beginning to discover how much interaction there is between body chemistry and emotional states. A disturbance in one area of the total person is likely to cause change in some other integral part.

If all this is true, we ought to be able to bring about the opposite effect and utilize our mind and soul to overcome some of the shortcomings of an afflicted body. We are integral creatures with a real need to understand our parts better if we are to learn to cope with them. Therefore, let me break away from my personal history for now, and explore how others cope with physical debilitation through emotional understanding and spiritual insight.

In his best-selling book *Anatomy of an Illness*, Norman Cousins reflects on his struggle with anklosing spondylitis, a degenerative disorder of the connective tissue in the spine which causes severe crippling and pain. His premise is that we play an active part in how our body relates to sickness. In other words, our recuperative processes can be affected by our attitude—even to the extent of changing the course of our disease.

Cousins refused to believe his own diagnosis was so bleak. He set about creating positive emotional experiences in an effort to reverse the life-threatening changes occurring in his body. If negative emotional stress can alter body chemistry, then a daily regimen of belly-laughter, coupled with good nutrition and carried out in a conducive environment, might bring about substantial change. (His reasoning has a sound base if we look at other physical disorders which often start from an *unhealthy* emotional environment.)

With the support of his doctor, he checked out of the hospital and into a hotel room. He surrounded himself with family and friends and hired private nurses to care for him. He prescribed for himself large doses of vitamin C, a good diet and a decrease in pain medication, especially aspirin. His Hollywood connections arranged the loan of old Marx brothers movies. Although it was months before a marked turning could be seen, Norman Cousins laughed himself out of pain and into recovery.

Some may say his victory holds no promise because his is an isolated case. Perhaps the disease would have ebbed on its own. Or maybe his mind took over, creating a placebo effect. In any case, the fact is that he recovered fully against one in 500 odds and seems to have had a whale of a time doing so.

True, most of us cannot afford the luxury of hotel

rooms, private nurses and room service. Few of us could call Hollywood and have Marx brothers films personally lent to us. Sadly, it is even difficult for the common person to find a doctor who would support such an unprecedented idea, especially when it is initiated by the patient.

But each of us can find some means to implement Cousins' *idea*. One way of gaining a measure of sanity in times like this is to learn how to adapt. If we can find alternate, practical ways of making our world seem worthwhile despite illness, half the battle is won.

I'm not just speaking about occupational therapists teaching you how to put your boat in the water without straining your back. I'm talking more about finding ways within yourself to fight back, to use what you do have to *overcome* what you lack not just compensate for it.

My father's stroke, for example, left him with a rare optical problem. The vision in his left eye fluttered from side to side while the vision in his right eye fluttered up and down. His doctors were baffled, saying this was physiologically impossible even though it was substantiated through testing. Their only suggestion was to patch one eye and have him make do as best he could with the other.

That was not good enough for my father. After weeks of sitting in his favorite chair on the front porch and thinking about this problem, my father started cutting black strips of paper and gluing them on his glasses—a few vertical lines on the left and a few horizontal lines on the right, varying in width and spacing. He had *on his own* figured out a way to block out some of the fluttering, thereby reducing the number of double images he was seeing. Though far from perfect, it succeeded in giving him a steadier world.

Each person must deal with illness in his or her own way. Though medical symptoms correspond to specific illnesses, the dimension of personal consequences depends greatly on individual circumstances. No two people suffer the same disease identically. No one but you will fully understand the extent of your difficulty and how it applies to your unique situation. No one else can make the move which, however small, enables you to reclaim your life.

I now believe that anything which helps us regain some lost vitality will fuel the fire, so to speak, and enable us to do that much more. I know these words may sound shallow and empty. I never cared much for such ideas either but, because I have found a grain of truth in them, I'll let them stand. You'll have to see for yourself if they help rebuild your world.

5

Coping With the Simple Things

Seeking ways to "live life to the fullest" and actually implementing these in our lives are often two entirely different matters. Furthermore, many of us simply *can't* find solutions on our own; we don't have the assets of a Norman Cousins or the creative mind of my father. Your affliction might not allow you the privilege of travel or even work. Maybe you have barely enough energy to make it through from dawn to dusk, let alone be inspired or inspiring. Personal finances may keep you in such straits you couldn't implement a good idea anyway. You get angry and frustrated that your best efforts fall so short of the much-needed mark. Where do you turn? How will you cope?

The first step is to talk over these frustrations and limitations with your friends or family. Hospitals, social agencies, special interest organizations and religious groups all supply various aids and services. Most clinics offer psychological counseling or family services such as child care, transportation, financial consultants, special long-term billing. But no one will know your needs if you don't mention them; no support can be utilized if you don't pursue it.

    I know of a crippled man whose dream was to serve Communion at our church. No one knew he was even interested until he mentioned to a friend that he was too embarrassed to volunteer because of the unsightly nicotine stains on his fingers and nails. Since his right arm was paralyzed, he was unable to attend to the proper cleaning of his left hand. In order to be a Eucharistic minister, he had to come up with a way to cleanse his left hand. Solution? His friend nailed a small brush securely to the bathroom shelf for him to scrub against, and his dream was fulfilled.

    Sound like a simple problem? From what I've seen it *is* the minor, annoying, inconvenient, daily limitations that really get people down. I know someone who was confined to a wheelchair. The person got "used to" that but secretly confided to me that one never gets "used to" the aggravation and humiliation of having to ask one's spouse for a portable container to urinate into. There are limits to the blows our self-esteem can take before we lose faith in who and what we are. These limits preserve our dignity and should be considered precious in both ourselves and others.

    To a sick or handicapped person the world is full of obstacles, setbacks, disappointments, indignities and frustrations. Even the strongest determination, if met with enough resistance, can falter. In college, I knew a blind student who worked diligently into his junior year—and then left school even though he was a B student. He could no longer emotionally cope with the daily aggravation of getting the materials he needed put into braille so that he could get his work in on time. It was not his handicap or the challenge that squelched his initiative, but the day-to-day stumbling blocks the college system put in front of him.

Helen Keller, in her book *Midstream*, says that it is not so much the missed sunset or blue skies, it is "the thousand petty restraints" that encompass a sightless person. "The hardest thing we bear is that we cannot go about the simplest matters of life alone. With all our hearts we desire to be strong, free, and useful."

Keller continues to remind the reader that her great success in overcoming her limitations was largely due to the love, dedication and ingenuity of Anne Sullivan, her tutor and lifelong companion. She writes that she was greatly humbled when she realized not everyone was as fortunate in misfortunes as she.

Most of us lack individual, daily assistance. Quite often we will be alone, left with our shortcomings while family and friends are working, shopping and doing other necessary things. Although we are grateful for their love and concern and for all they do for us, their *doing* only increases our own feeling of worthlessness as our inadequacy looms before us.

Such feelings of worthlessness and inadequacy sap a great deal of our emotional energy and sabotage our best efforts at adaptation. They leave us angry and further withdrawn, convinced all the more of our useless state. Until my illness, I never understood why sick people didn't *do something* rather than just *sit there* in front of the TV. It was only during my own incapacity that I realized the paralyzing effect of inactivity—it seems inactivity breeds more inactivity. There comes a time in prolonged illness when the fact of being disabled becomes a handicap in itself, *a preoccupation with being unable.* The day becomes one long reminder of all that you can no longer do.

With my own back problem I "got used" to not being active; I tried to do what I could in my reduced mobility. But if no one was around and I had to forego lunch or postpone finishing a vital task because I couldn't stretch to reach the proper ingredients, utensils or whatever, I became angry. In the four years my father lived after his stroke, it was the little things he once could do in a jiffy—like threading a line through the eyes of a fishing pole—that infuriated him and often were tossed aside in an abandoned heap.

This type of anger is called "displacement." We are *really* angry at being disabled, but we know there is very little we can do about that. So we strike out at a lesser foe. The classic example of displaced anger is the person who comes home from a bad day at work and snaps at a spouse who scolds a child who kicks the dog.

We can fall into many *negative* adaptations. Tucking my hand in my jeans pocket and tying my arm to my hip were both negative adaptations. They didn't serve to strengthen my arm; my rationalizing only served as denial. Similarly, a friend rearranged her house—moving her bedroom downstairs—so she could do *less* exercise on her sore hip following hip replacement surgery instead of *more* exercise as the doctor ordered. This negative adaptation has hindered her recovery to the extent that she now walks with an aggravated limp.

Another friend had bypass surgery. Doctors recommended he maintain a specific weight and get plenty of exercise, but my friend did just the opposite: He gained plenty of weight, thereby curbing his ability to exercise and leaving him short of breath. Through a negative adaptation, he proceeded to till his beloved garden on hands and knees. When confronted, my friend remarked, "It's easier to see the weeds when I'm kneeling."

What fragile creatures we are! There are circumstances that we cannot alter. Negative adaptations such as displaced anger and denial are very understandable reactions to difficult situations. But sooner or later we need to leave them behind. There *is* plenty we can do afterwards to reclaim our lives—if we try to face ourselves.

6

Admitting Fear

It is difficult at best for any of us to admit that we are less able than we were. Everyone around us sees it. We are the last to recognize our negative adaptations for what they really are: expressions of fear. We are afraid to give in, even a little, lest our self-identity crumble. All our lives we strive to be independent, and illness leads to dependence. It therefore leads to feelings of inadequacy which we cannot cure with a pill or a shot in the arm.

Being dependent is especially devastating for a family breadwinner, a mother of small children, an essential executive—people who have reason to fear for their dependents as well as for themselves. Luckily, no one depended on me. My fears were for myself.

I found it very difficult at times to explain these fears to those around me, let alone feel that they understood. I not only feared the decline in my health and all its implications for my life, but I very humanly began to fear some of the diagnostic procedures, treatments and drugs to which I was subjected.

All of this is part of the inevitable psychological regression we go through when we are sick. This regression can be especially difficult to handle if we are used to seeing ourselves as competent and successful. Our dependency makes us vulnerable. Suddenly things we were never concerned about, things we had never given much thought to, loom threateningly before us. For example, *angiogram* is a word we know has something to do with diagnosing coronary disease. It's quite a different matter, though, when they're going to insert a needle into *your* artery.

When we are well, we protect ourselves from thinking about such things; we discuss them with great detachment. We are safe. We are healthy. But sickness can bring with it all kinds of procedures that can seem worse than the illness itself. Furthermore, we can't really imagine what some tests are like, so our psychological preparation may miss the mark. Sometimes we are pleasantly surprised and breathe a sigh of relief after a test which wasn't so bad after all. But other times the tests themselves can be very difficult to cope with, despite the assurances of technicians and physicians. Sadly, some tests and treatments need not be as uncomfortable as they are.

I have a very vivid memory of unnecessary discomfort. During my back treatment, I had to have an EMG (electromyogram). "It doesn't hurt a bit," I was told by one physician. Mind you, this test sends an electric impulse from a metallic probe (inserted into a muscle) along a specific nerve path. How can such a test *not* hurt? Especially when they are inserting this metal probe 20 times or so along your neck, spine, fingers and face?

The first time was bad enough; but then, about a year later I had to have another one. Almost in tears, I told the new doctor, "There is no way I am having another one of those tests." My distress was evident, so he scheduled my appointment with the team who gives EMG's at a nearby children's hospital.

The difference between these two tests was like night and day. The first had been given under bright fluorescent lights in a corner of a busy physical therapy room on a cold, hard table. The doctor had communicated with his instrument panel more than with me.

The second was given in a softly lighted private room. The room was very warm, even hot, which was explained as a way to keep the muscles relaxed so the insertion of the probe wouldn't hurt so much. The table had a pillow and a blanket so I could lie comfortably and hug the blanket for security. The second physician talked me through the entire procedure. I knew each time he was going to stick me with the probe, each time he was going to twist it to locate the nerve, each time he was going to increase the current to get a good reading. Perhaps the most settling thing he did was to place his hand on each spot for a few seconds before he inserted the probe. He told me it helped warm and relax the muscle; it also helped relieve my anxiety. The second test, consequently, was not nearly as traumatic as the first. It hurt, but the pain seemed less because of all the personal care taken to put me at ease. I wouldn't be afraid to take another EMG from this second doctor, but I would never recommend someone go through what I did at the first hospital.

Patients sometimes think the doctor knows everything. In this case, the first prescribing doctor didn't even know the physician who gave what ended up being a painful test. When I went back and told him how well the *second* test went, he was very grateful for the information and said he'd be careful where he sent his patients. It was as if my experience was the first *personal* experience he had had with the treatment. Had I said nothing, countless patients would still be needlessly subjected to a bad experience.

We are all different, and one person's sensitivity may or may not be the same as another's. Because of these individual variations it is important to find a physician you trust and are comfortable with. It makes no sense to *endure* relationships (even professional ones) if someone else can bring satisfaction instead of dread.

Of the 15 or 20 doctors who poked around on my back, I can tell you that only one or two were sensitive to my pain. For some reason, the others seemed heavy-handed, more intent on their need to examine me than my need to be examined gently, thoroughly, effectively. My primary physician at the Pain Control Center was almost always tuned in to how painful my knotted, spastic muscles were. He very conscientiously used thinner needles in the most sensitive areas so as not to irritate the muscles more.

One time, however, I needed treatment and my doctor was out of town. Another staff doctor was called in to give me an injection on the back of my neck. The nurse reminded him that a thinner needle "might be better," but he had a thick one already prepared. Believe me, it may not have made much difference to him but it surely did to me.

Actually, I have been lucky. My treatments were nothing like the ordeals faced by people in certain drug therapies, radiation treatments, burn centers, etc. In any case, we don't have to be ashamed of feeling afraid. We have a right to the way we feel. And even though we may try to cover our fear with masks of anger, withdrawal, denial or belligerence, we are basically trying to escape the feeling of inadequacy and the terror it evokes. Once we recognize this, we can bring our creative imagination to these situations and make a small, but significant statement that, though we are sick, we still count as worthwhile people. We may feel unable to cope with the test, the pain, the stress, or bodily decline but we are human beings still; we deserve to be treated with dignity and respect.

The dehumanizing world of medicine provides us ample opportunities to work through such feelings. We are poked and probed in places we'd rather not be by people we barely know. We are dressed up in nondescript gowns (when we're lucky) that advertise us as "Hospital Property. Do Not Remove." No wonder we feel degraded!

But there is no way for people around us to tend our inner needs if all we ever present is stoic, self-contained assurance. Some perceptive people may see through such fronts and soothe the frightened inner self. But there are so few of these people in our lives, so few who can read our emotional needs better than we can read them ourselves. More often, no one hears our inner cry.

All of us hope that hospital and medical personnel will be more sensitive than lay people. How much easier it is for us when they are! Professionals are only human, though. No matter how fine their credentials or their reputation, they all have individual quirks, problems and fears. Their very professionalism can make them seem cold and aloof.

The poet Robert Frost, in a talk given at Berkeley in 1956, called this problem a matter of point of view. He pointed out that a doctor who loses a few cases every year experiences only a small loss, say, five percent. But to each of those patients and to their family and friends, the loss is 100 percent. Quite a difference in viewpoint!

As patients, we can try to make certain our point of view is acknowledged and understood by those who help us. This is not to say it will always be accepted, even by the most caring and considerate doctor. But at least it might be incorporated, if only partially, into our treatment plan. Getting around the defense mechanisms of some professionals may be difficult. Sadly, the professional you have a problem with may look upon it as your problem, thus protecting himself or herself from responsibility.

I say these things not to demean medicine or the people who have dedicated their lives to helping the sick. Rather, I speak for the thousands who live in silent awe of highly educated, specialized people who seem so much more healthy, happy and financially stable than "we" are. Our decline in health and ability can make us feel like second-rate citizens if we allow it to threaten our sense of individual worth. We are people who want mutual respect and a sense of connection but who are sometimes left feeling like a number, a case, a study or a diagnosis.

Our fears and our vulnerability are very much tied up with our self-esteem. Under the duress of sickness, we need to concentrate on health and wholeness, not fear. Opening our hearts and minds to honest communication with ourselves and those around us just might take the edge off of our anxiety, especially if the medical personnel around us try to respond to our plea.

7

Reaching Out for Support

Sickness brings yet another fear, one which is often more severe and even less talked about. This is the fear of how family and friends may begin to feel toward you for being sick. I learned this from both sides—as patient and as loving bystander—so I'm going to talk out of both sides of my mouth in this chapter.

Illness places a strain on a marriage, on family ties, friendships and business relationships. What do you do? Blame yourself? Blame God? Berate yourself because you didn't exercise more, relax more, stop smoking or drinking, take better care of yourself? Most of us do blame and berate, or are at least tempted to.

Being sick is not easy; we tend to resent the health of those around us. Living with the sick is not easy either. Stress comes from many directions, sometimes from those we least expect.

For example, I wanted to be supportive in my father's illness. At the same time I frequently wanted to run away and hide. It can be particularly hard to watch a parent's decline because no matter how old we are, at some level we still look to parents for strength and safety. And all of a sudden that parental shield is gone. It's hard to admit to yourself you are fearful of your own future when you feel that your first concern should be for this person who needs all your love and support.

The trial a spouse goes through may be even more difficult: returning love to someone who no longer looks or acts like the person you married—especially if the relationship isn't bonded with years of happiness and devotion. Yet being sick doesn't mean your emotions have quieted. More than ever you need closeness and presence, and there may be no easy way for your husband or wife to reach out to give you that kind of care.

In my own experience as the patient, plenty of conversations have started with guys and girls alike whose enthusiasm for friendship waned rapidly when I explained that I couldn't possibly go rafting or skiing or dancing, or play tennis, or sit through a whole play. I learned to stop saying, "But maybe we could do something else sometime," because there isn't a whole lot else to do except sit around and talk about everything you'd love to be doing. I looked healthy; so, I think, a lot of people mistook my refusal of their invitation as a brush-off. The face of pain is deceptive.

It is nice to come home from the hospital and have friends drop over or offer to cook or shop for you. But a long-term disease or problem that will keep you nursing for years is a far different thing. People begin to avoid you—and that's painful emotionally.

It can be even worse if you are physically disfigured and can't go anywhere without being on display. I vividly remember seeing a young boy grimace as my father staggered by with his stroke-damaged gait. The scene struck me deeply; my father was going to live in this little boy's mind as a kind of monster, a frightening thing, something to be avoided.

Maybe it is the child in our adult selves that flees from such encounters, too. We should be mature enough to focus our emotional reaction beyond the appearance of a hobbling man with a withered arm and black stripes gridding his glasses. But how many of us at some time couldn't bring ourselves to visit a dying friend because we just couldn't bear to see him or her "like that"?

It is imperative for us to remember that avoidance doesn't necessarily mean that people don't care anymore; rather they may care too much. It is hard for many people to express care and affection. They get so torn up inside for their dear, irreplaceable friend or loved one that they simply avoid the whole emotional web. Sometimes this web is strung with guilt, sometimes with feelings of inadequacy, an inability to help, hopelessness, the staggering reality that the same thing could happen to them.

I once asked some friends why they had stopped dropping by a mutual acquaintance's house after he became sick. Our friend was long since dead at this point, but I wondered why they had abruptly stopped going. They told me they couldn't bring themselves to visit him; it was so sad. I knew what they were saying, but I also knew our friend's isolation and bitterness might have been lessened had they stopped to see him. In his mind, their absence was chalked up as insincerity; they were fair-weather friends who didn't really care at all. I can only wonder how different both parties might have felt if they had had the occasion to share *their* pain.

Sometimes organizations can help. A parish prayer group or other organization which meets frequently can offer support. There are national support groups concerned with particular diseases and handicaps — cancer victims and their families, for example. But the right organization may not even exist in your town. If your problem is a less well-known illness, public awareness can be devastatingly small. You can feel totally alone, overwhelmed by something which, before your illness, didn't seem remotely possible.

As much as we need people around us to care for our needs, we have to accept the fact that they have needs too. Certainly they lay aside many of their needs in caring for us, but the danger lies in putting them at risk of sickness themselves, emotional or physical.

Even the most caring people need time to get away and relax. Giving them that freedom once in a while is a good way to insure their ability to keep on giving to us. This will take real planning and understanding. I think it has to be a scheduled thing, not something squeezed in between meeting our needs or put off until we are feeling better. Our needs may never be met. We may never feel better.

The degree that our sickness affects our life or someone else's cannot be measured by some objective standard. Each situation is different. Therefore people must assess their own strengths and weaknesses to evaluate the amount and type of help they will need to cope. It is a learning process, at times trial and error, but given enough time, enough ways to divert tension, enough love and concern, most needs can be met—sometimes even comfortably.

For instance, a friend's brother lost all his hair during chemotherapy. His sister dressed him up in a wig and makeup so people in the restaurants and stores of their chic California suburb would think he was a rock star instead of a dying young man. I'm sure the hilarity of being mistaken for an entertainment personality eased the terror he masked so bravely. As tragic as mortality can be, when we display in its face, even for the tiniest moment, our resilience and courage, we see humanity at its finest.

No example stands clearer in my mind than my young cousin Michelle. She suffered from birth with a rare, incurable muscular dysfunction which left her confined to a wheelchair and then to a bed for nearly all her 15 years. Her daily existence required a special car to travel in, air-filtering systems to keep down germs and aid in her breathing, special devices to help her type a letter, turn pages in a book. Her family loved her dearly; without them she could not have lived as long and as well as she did. Wise beyond her years, she housed in a frail and deformed body a spirit that puts mine to shame. In a will written several years before she died, she wrote a phrase that appeared on the memorial card at her funeral: "Remember me in happiness; otherwise don't remember me at all."

8

Working Through the Stages

People like Michelle are few and far between. Most of us don't even face the flu or a sore throat without lapsing into a little depression or self-pity. Few of us could face an entire life of sickness with such courage—even happiness—unto death. Yet sickness and death are in all our lives; if we could learn from people like Michelle, maybe it all would be a little less painful.

In a way, I think all sickness is like death, even the sicknesses we recover from. Like the dying, we don't function or feel well physically. We exhibit signs of bodily distress: fever, nausea, vomiting, pain, weakness. We also experience feelings of anxiety, dependence, separation, loss. In certain illnesses, even aspects of the course of treatment parallel death.

Undergoing general anesthesia is a common example. For many people anesthesia is a terrifying state of suspension they fear they will never come back from. Being wheeled away from friends and family into an operating room full of masked doctors and nurses, bright lights and sterile machinery is often experienced as the *last* thing they will ever see. Being so vulnerable, seeing the world from a prone position, being draped in sheets on a hospital dolly like a corpse—all this is understandably frightening. Most of us will experience or witness situations like this at some point in our lives. Though most of us will recover—most will "come back"—none of us is exempt from sickness, aging and death.

Why is it, then, that some people (like Michelle) cope with a harsh destiny so much better than others? Is it just a matter of individual intestinal fortitude? Or is it that, when confronted with the emotional maze that accompanies all illness, people like Michelle transcend while others get trapped? We get lost in one emotional phase or another—in anger or guilt, confusion or despair. If we are stuck in such a mind-set, our time and energy are certainly not focused constructively. Instead, we while away our energy in anger, remorse or withdrawal.

It is difficult to move out of such a mind-set, but not impossible. Elisabeth Kubler-Ross, in her book *On Death and Dying*, names and explores the stages of dying: denial, anger, bargaining, depression and, finally, acceptance. If we view illness as a tiny experience of death, then we can see that we pass through like stages in sickness. The length and intensity of each stage depends on who we are, what our life experience has been. Our reactions are specific to our personal histories and individual psychological makeup.

If we are aware of these stages, we see when our emotions are snagged. We can work with the people around us to be free. Somewhere in the passage of time, we will reach resolution, either in despair or in acceptance. Harnessing our emotional energy can be a driving force in regaining our own productivity. Leaving it unharnessed, untapped, can lead to the further decay of the individual. The choice is more ours than it might seem.

We can all cite instances where one person has a bright, optimistic attitude and someone else gives up even though they both have equally debilitating illnesses or injuries. Sickness can be likened to a hammer: If it hits a fly, the fly dies; if it hits an elephant, the elephant won't even wince. Sickness, and its accompanying decline, hits people in much the same way—only it can turn flies into elephants and elephants into flies. We don't know how we will react until it is upon us. We can only hope and work toward acceptance, toward making the very best of the situation. We can strive toward those things we think we can change and we must learn to accept the inevitable.

Foremost, however, is learning the difference between the two. Acceptance, as a peaceful resolution of certain circumstances, can be a *beginning*, not only an end. For example, I know of an elderly man who was given six months to live. He could have chosen to stay home in England and see his illness through till death. Instead he packed up his bags and flew to Assisi where he has lived for 10 years offering room and board to young travelers.

Similarly, a widow I know didn't succumb to the

mundane life of her small Midwest town when her husband died. She flew to Israel to work in an orphanage. At 73 she discovered she had breast cancer. When she had to travel to a distant city for radium treatment, she spent her days working in a local soup kitchen.

In the book *Renoir: His Life, Art and Letters*, Barbara White tells us how the great, gentle painter suffered so severely from rheumatoid arthritis that his brushes had to be strapped to his hand, yet he painted 100 pictures in the last five years of his life.

Many circumstances over which we have no control can bring us to the point of helplessness. It is what we do from that point on that culminates in human triumph or defeat.

9
Facing Mortality

During the years I walked and sat in the cemetery, I thought a lot about mortality and how it fits into things. I thought a lot about what life really means if all that is left of most of our stories is a dash chiseled between two dates. At times I remembered what a friend of mine, a student of Tibetan Buddhism, had told me: Before entering religious life, the monks meditate on their burial sites, open fields of unburied carrion. Far from bringing despair, their insights cleanse them of earthly possessiveness, free them for a feeling of nothingness—a nothingness full of spirit, light and peace, unweighted by earthly shackles.

    I compared these Eastern monks to myself and to the people around me. Finally I realized why it is so difficult for Americans to reach such acceptance of death. We in the West have life in abundance. The daily business of ensuring physical survival is generally easier here than in most countries of the world. Far from being taught to strive for a feeling of wonder in nothingness we are encouraged to want almost everything—and we want those everythings made easy. Our whole society is geared to go faster, higher, sooner, better than anybody else.

The rate at which our knowledge and scientific advances are mushrooming is staggering. Whereas it took millenia even to learn the techniques of flight, we put a man on the moon in a quarter of a century after our first invasion of space.

Medical science has advanced by leaps and bounds in the past 50 years, especially with the introduction of antibiotics, vaccines against many diseases, improved surgical techniques and vast new areas of medical specialties. The probability of a viral cure is on the horizon. With that an entire new dimension of cure will arrive: The common cold well might taunt us no more; cancer might at last be checked. Perhaps we truly are racing toward *Star Trek* technology, when a small beeping ball passed above our bodies will diagnose us and invasive surgery will be completely replaced by a laser beam.

Such creative imagination lays the path for the rest of us to follow. We have the power to form the future by setting a goal "out there," giving it flesh with our imaginations. Sooner or later, as technologists strive to actualize the idea, the future is born in the present. And we with our space suits and our almost magic technology will be as gods to our own past. Technology is in essence the mind giving birth to itself, idea becoming fact. It is self-perpetuating. It is good. It is right and seems to be part of the natural order of things.

Our 20th century seems to be an age so oriented toward the future that we don't want to look back. In a society marked by high technology, computerization, mass media, rapid transit and telecommunications, we sense the dynamic excitement of the world around us. We don't want to think of ourselves as slowing down, stopping, dying, ending the effervescence of life. It is hard to have to "take a back seat"; it makes one feel like an unnecessary part rather than a vital constituent.

Who gets lost in this space-age shuffle? Those people who are "in the way," those people who "hold us back," those people who remind us that it all will end: the sick, the indigent, the incapacitated, the elderly.

One example of this unsettling reality is the viewpoint which sees the natural process of aging as a disaster, as a time of medical expense, illness, sadness and uselessness instead of a time for wisdom, experience, knowledge, contentment, family position and love. Do we put our aging relatives into homes in the misguided belief that since science has offered us so much hope in its dogged pursuit of other cures, surely doctors and nurses can help us now? But there is no cure for old age. There is no escaping death.

Kubler-Ross tells us that our unconscious conviction is that we will live forever. We cannot accept the thought of our personal demise, but only that of someone else. In past generations the reality of death was incorporated and recognized as part of life. People died at home, wakes were held in the parlor; children and family were involved in the preparations, etc.

The current mind-set is determination to shield the children, the patient and the family from the unavoidable, often gruesome reality of human mortality. We dress up the dead and tell the children they're asleep. We house the dying in institutions, ICU's and hospital rooms even though many would prefer to go home and die in peace. Kubler-Ross continues, "If we now look at our society, we may want to ask ourselves what happens to the individual in a society bent on ignoring or avoiding death?" And, "Maybe the question has to be raised: Are we becoming less human or more human?...It is clear that whatsoever the answer may be, the patient is suffering more—not physically, perhaps, but emotionally. And the needs have not changed over the centuries, only our ability to gratify them."

If ever there was a need for change, for some inward focus, the time is now. For as humankind strives better to understand and elevate itself, its main propulsion becomes a steady focus on "out there," upon the *mechanics* of human life and its surroundings.

In contrast to this is our human condition. Though technology can be empirically measured, the human spirit cannot. We are fragile vessels needing an inward focus as well, some resting place where humility lives. Here lies true knowledge: No matter how advanced or far-reaching our achievements, we will never be anything more than what we were created and intended to be. Our achievements are only a reflection of the great Achiever, our intelligence only a fleeting thought compared to the one unifying Intelligence, our life but one breath in all of life.

For me, feeling the frailty of mortality was the beginning of my awareness of soul. Adaptations and attitudes—these things I could usually muster out of sheer inner determination. But accepting my condition, my limitedness, was for me a fundamental step toward the beginning of humility: knowing who I wasn't, in the light of the One who is.

10

Discovering Our Creaturehood

I feel a turning point in my thoughts here. After laying down background experiences and the consequences of my bodily decline, after bringing in examples of myself and others to present an overall grasp of coping as a whole, I'm going to turn away from physical and mental generalities and focus on a different viewpoint: our spirituality.

The word *spiritual* has many connotations. Like the Greek *arete*, it is an encompassing term—one that may or may not include religion. I believe the thrust for wholeness is reflective of one's spirit. Most anyone agrees such vibrance is a healthy, positive sign. I doubt, however, that most of the people I have mentioned ascribe any specific religious significance to their recuperative process, their coping or, in some cases, their remaining illness. But I personally could never write on this subject without including some thoughts on my own understanding of the religious dimension.

I don't like delving into the spiritual power within us for several reasons—mainly because I don't think most of us see ourselves as spiritually powerful in any sense of the word. We so often associate spiritual power with saints or famous TV healers; we forget our own worth and capabilities. We forget that the good in our lives, the vitality of relationships, love, enjoyment are all reflections of the wholeness intended for us by God.

What spiritual power I do sense in myself stems from my understanding of who we are in reference to God. We are the created beings and he is the Creator, the sole life-giver. This relationship I experience profoundly, probably because of my kinship with nature. Your relationship, your experience of God may be different. I think these things are as individual as fingerprints.

Meister Eckhart, a 13th-century theologian and preacher highly attuned to the meaning of creaturehood, wrote, "God in creating all creatures instructs and enjoins, advises and commands them, by the very fact that he creates them, to follow him and conform themselves to him, to turn and hasten back to him as the first cause of their entire being...." In *Breakthrough*, a commentary on Eckhart's creation spirituality, Matthew Fox continues, "While all creation has flowed out from God according to the image that God held of things in the creative mind and while wisdom and goodness have been created in a very special way according to what flows from himself, the soul is yet greater and more God-like."

We, creatures and creation all, are part of God's

nature and as such have been given the privilege to be like him, to use all that he has given us in order to draw closer to him. Creation spirituality further implies that everything we experience, God experienced first. If this were not so, then we could not think, feel, hear, touch, mourn, love, cry, laugh. God encompasses all things. Outside of him there is nothing. Within him exists all things: good and evil, happiness and sadness, life and death. This is not to say that God *created* or *is* both; rather, that in him all things exist—even things we assume he doesn't like.

If we cry, it is because God cried first—as he reminds us through his prophet Hosea. If we grieve at the loss of a loved one, it is because God first grieved when the creature most like his own self—the creature he loved and lavished Paradise on, the creature he gave free will so it would know it was truly free and alive—turned against him and was lost by its own doing, its own choice.

Thus, God is like a parent who has given a child every possible happiness and security, showered him or her with love and companionship only to have the youngster want more, to be an equal instead of a cherished child. And the parent has to stand by and watch, offer counsel and direction, hope and plan for the best, all the while in pain and sorrow as the child goes headlong in the one single misdirection when a world of infinite right directions is already available.

If we feel empathy for one another and reach out with our hearts and talents to help, it is because God leaps within us. This is not to say that we will never experience harsh, brutal existence, for we have. But even in such an existence, there lies a desire, both in him and in us, for peace. What we need is a healing experience, an immersion of self into wholeness. We need to travel to that healing place within, especially when such a place does not exist without.

One very touching story of someone with a valiant inner focus concerns a young friend of a priest I know. This Swiss teenager was dying of a fast-acting bone cancer. Barely able to walk, he dragged himself up the steep Alpine landscape to scavenge through the crags of his mountain for the elusive edelweiss blossom. Edelweiss grows on the sunny side of rocks above 7,000 feet, between the snow and the runoff to the grasses below. He found the flower. Back from the mountain, he gave it to my friend to remember him by and died shortly thereafter.

I cannot help but think that when we enter the doors of a pain clinic, intensive care unit, psychiatric ward, alcohol rehabilitation center, nursing home or any such place where we find ourselves seemingly without recourse, we somehow have to believe the edelweiss is there. *It* is what is important, even if we die pursuing it. And it is only by entering in and working through the process day-by-day, week-by-week with family, friends and knowledgeable professionals—mortal beings all—that we make an unexpected discovery: We are the edelweiss.

11

Understanding God's Will

As we read through the Gospels, we see clearly that Jesus does not tolerate sickness or, at times, even death. In 34 specific encounters with sick people, he heals all of them. This doesn't include the dozens, maybe thousands of other healings grouped together as "crowds," "townspeople," "all who were present," etc. He rebukes his own disciples for not healing the sick. He despairs at how long he must put up with their dullness, their failure to see that the power to heal lies within them. He tires of their continued reluctance to believe that the Father wishes to see his people whole and at peace.

If we look at Jesus' life, we learn he doesn't doubt for a minute his Father's desire to see us totally healed. It wasn't good enough that the blind man at Bethsaida could see men who "looked like trees." Jesus continued praying until the blind man saw men who looked like men (see Mark 8:22-26).

Jesus, the image of the Father, tells us to be perfect as our heavenly Father is perfect (see Matthew 5:48). Jesus tells us to love God and to love one another as ourselves (see Luke 10:27), and to love as perfectly as he has loved us (see John 15:12). I think too often we take this to mean we are to *be good*. Most of us would see this as an impossibility, for there is no way we are always going to be good. Jesus clears up this misconception by telling us only the Father is good (see Luke 18:19). We think of "good" as a measure of performance. Love, however, is the action of giving, of self-sacrifice irrespective of result. It is not a measured performance, it is a lifelong effort, a willingness to try. St. Augustine tells us how incredible life would be if we loved even the *idea* of love.

What happened to the perfect oneness with God Jesus urges his followers to have? One of the signs Jesus says will accompany his disciples is the ability to heal the sick. We are his followers, yet when was the last time we healed someone or raised a body from death? The early Christians seemed to expect such happenings as a matter of course. James urges the sick to come before the elders for prayer and anointing and to expect healing. Today we seem to have reduced healing from the rule to the exception. I cannot help but wonder if this is why we seem so powerless in our daily dealings with one another: We don't believe we can heal or be healed.

How does the belief that God doesn't really intend for us to be well get imbedded in our minds and paralyze our faith? How does this trickle of doubt grow until we are flooded with hesitation, disbelief and discouragement to the point that we relegate what once was the commonplace to the miraculous?

One reason it happens is that our notion of God is so limited. We always try to understand God on our own terms. But Jesus came to correct our misconceptions about his Father and to enlarge our perspective.

He was the new Adam restoring to us the inheritance of grace and power which was ours as children of the Kingdom and heirs of the Father. He tells us that we must be reborn; and in that new birth, we will find life.

Being reborn, however, is not easy. We must find inside of ourselves inner expanses and new depths of courage. We must see our earthly experience as our *rite du passage.* Our entering in and our emergence from mortality is like the native Americans' going into their ceremonial kiva—a partially submerged, womblike structure—and coming out a "new" person.

Every day, as we transcend strife and through our human struggle bring about new life, we are reborn and God is reborn through us and in us. This rebirthing process is painful. It is difficult to grasp. Not part of God's original plan, it is necessary for our redemption because of original sin.

I am no theologian. I cannot outline the progression of thought that leads from our birth in the Garden to the distinction between God's permissive and perfect will—the latter his ideal plan before Adam's sin and the former what he chooses to sit back and watch happen since the fall. (That distinction has been, however, very helpful to me at times.)

I only know that all people suffer sickness, pain and

death. Though I do not doubt that some suffering is redemptive, I see this as the exception rather than the rule. In God's perfect will there was no need for suffering or redemption at all. I certainly don't think God planned for my father to have a stroke at age 50 and suffer complication upon complication until he finally died. I think this is part of God's permissive will, happenings which God tried to spare us by giving us the Garden to live in. Likewise, I do not believe that any being who could create something as magnificent as a Canada goose would want to see it brought down by a crippled foot or a broken wing.

Another reason for our preoccupation with suffering and our lack of belief in healing is that we overidentify with Christ's crucifixion and death instead of his resurrection.

Growing up among Catholic friends, I do not remember the name of Jesus being associated with healing. For example, when I was afraid of the dentist's drill, I was told I should think of Jesus and all the pain he suffered for us on the cross, rather than all the healing he wanted to give me.

I think this is a very real attitude among Christians: Jesus felt pain for us, so we should feel pain for him. This kind of logic is like parents working their whole lives to make a safe, secure world for their children, only to see them refuse to live in it because they think the *struggle* is the point. All that the parents "killed themselves for" is set aside, misunderstood and unused, because the children fail to realize it is in the gift that their happiness lies.

We should cultivate the awareness of the gift itself rather than the pain associated with it. We have nothing to lose. How safe it is for us, really, to use the gift, to act in Jesus' name. If you think about it, it is like taking a blueprint to someone and saying, "The architect asked me to give this to you, so if it doesn't work, don't blame me!" We need not feel like failures if we pray and the prayer goes unanswered. Our only job is to believe enough to ask and to keep on asking should we begin to disbelieve. Jesus' words defend his works, not ours.

12

Praying for Healing

What does it mean to pray in Jesus' name? Does it mean we tack "In the name of Jesus, amen" to the end of all our prayers and they will automatically come true? To answer this question we must look at the significance of a name when Jesus used it. In biblical times someone's name was an all-encompassing referral to the person's personality. A name was more than an appellation; it reflected who the person was. So when we pray in Jesus' name, we are to pray as he prayed, trying to grasp his feelings, his belief, his compassion.

The *manner* of his praying is extremely important. Some human interaction is usually connected with his healings. He doesn't just utter a silent prayer. He goes to people or they come to him. He talks to them or addresses their sickness directly. Frequently he *touches* the sick (or they touch him) and the illness leaves.

Ashley Montagu, famous author and teacher at Harvard, New York University and Rutgers, says in his book *Touching*, "The skin, like a cloak, covers all of us all over, the oldest and the most sensitive of our organs, our first medium of communication....The sense of touch [is] 'the mother of the senses.' "

Jesus was human as well as divine. He had been raised at his mother's breast. He knew tenderness and warmth. In working with Joseph as a carpenter, he learned that the greatest tool a carpenter has is his hands. They were surer even than the eye in sanding down a finish or smoothing out a line.

I don't think we should find it surprising that he reached out and touched the sick or that they were compelled to reach out and touch him. We touch one another all the time: a handshake, a slap on the back, a pat on the head, hugs of joy, love and sorrow. But how many of us would walk over to our neighbor's sickbed and ask if we could rest our hands on him or her while we pray?

For some reason the idea—even the words "laying on of hands"—conjures up all sorts of ambivalent attitudes in people. Even though we recognize the comfort touch brings, we are often hindered from combining it with prayer because of "what people might think." Similarly, even if those who offer prayer overcome *their* reservations, the sick person may still be reluctant to accept such an offer—much less to invite it.

It does little good to offer the presence of God's healing love to others only to have them so "turned off" they never want any part of religion again. Sadly, this happens when we force the point, embarrass another or appear to belittle someone else's faith.

Is this why we shy away from healing prayer—because we have all seen people using religion in ways that are uncomfortable to us? I didn't want to go to that prayer meeting back in college because I was afraid of what kind of nuts those people must be if they sat around and prayed every Thursday night. That was okay for ministers, priests, or nuns—but not for "ordinary" people.

Religion can be abused in many ways. An example would be to believe in no healing but faith healing. I know of someone who was a devout Christian in a mainline denominational Church. This individual refused medical care, believing God would heal the illness, until the pain reached such levels of intensity that the person committed suicide. If we can misunderstand Jesus to such a sad extreme as this, no wonder there is so little spiritual healing in our lives.

Paramount in praying for another is remembering that we are not offering anything of our own making. We should pray that the person receive, receive, receive—for the power has been given, if only we can muddle through, utilizing it as best we can.

I witnessed a moving example, simply and effectively done, while visiting a friend in England. He had just learned his daughter was epileptic and wondered how he could best pray over her. A devout Anglican, he believed Jesus would want to see his daughter healed. He didn't want to frighten her in any way, for she was already understandably fearful of the seizures and the restrictions they placed on her young life. He knew the value of laying his hands on her as Christ did; so he sat down on the sofa and talked to his child, explaining his feelings and hesitations. They agreed that whenever she snuggled close to him on the couch—watching TV, reading or whatever—it would be understood that he might be silently praying for her.

This is just one example of how people can put one another at ease in a very low-key yet efficacious way. You should be prudent and understanding, for though touch is important, it is not imperative. So if it seems you're going to cause problems by suggesting it—don't.

The concept of spiritual healing can be a pretty tough thing for Catholics to accept. Such notions were once associated with pentecostal gatherings and sideshow cajoling to "step forward and be saved." Yet Catholics have always sought healing through sacraments, novenas or the intercession of a saint. And, indeed, God *does* heal through sacraments, novenas and saints' intercessions. But God also heals in Spirit-filled gatherings, too.

We should remember that when Peter told Jesus that people not of their group were using his name to bring about healings, Jesus told Peter to let them be for their works were proof enough that they were not against him but for him (see Mark 9:38-40). In the end, the important thing to realize is that God heals in many ways.

I also think it is only common sense to pray with people as their receptivity dictates. For instance, another friend's mother was very active in her parish, involved in Cursillo, Marriage Encounter, a prayer group, etc. When she developed cancer, she welcomed her friends' praying over her. In fact, a group of people kept a regular prayer schedule while she underwent six months of treatment. She came through the chemotherapy with flying colors and almost no side effects at all.

I personally have been greatly influenced by Barbara Shlemon's *Healing Prayer*. In it she offers a terrific way to pray for healing without the person knowing you are praying at all. This can be especially helpful in a delicate situation. Her approach is to envision the person for whom we pray inside our own heart, surrounded by care and love. She suggests we bring this image into us daily for a given time, and try to picture the person free of affliction.

However we choose to pray for healing, we should be confident enough to pray in Jesus' name, yet humble enough to accept God's will. We should be gentle yet firm enough to see it through—like Jesus praying for the blind man twice. We should be willing yet prudent enough to be discreet and empathetic as when Jesus raised the dead woman, keeping everyone else outside. We must accept ourselves in our sinful, broken states as worthwhile vehicles of grace to others and as worthy objects of others' prayers. We must reeducate our minds toward acceptance of a loving, present God who gives to us and wants us to give his love to each other. In that exchange, accomplished through quiet prayer and gentle touch, we offer the love within ourselves in his name.

13

Overcoming Evil

Often just suggesting that others should pray for us can reinforce an erroneous but common notion that we are sick because we are somehow bad and therefore require the intercession of good people to heal us.

I still shudder when I remember the friend who prayed over my back and then told me my pain was the result of an evil presence residing in me. The last thing I needed at that time was for someone to imply in any way that I was somehow evil. No matter how well-intended such things are or how thought out the theology, likening sickness to evil will *not* be taken by a sick person as a cosmic reference but as a personal one. I felt evil enough already, being so humanly angry and frustrated. Lord knows I was in enough black moods from day-to-day discomfort that it truly seemed like some monster reigned within. I did not need it likened to spirits and devils.

Though I do not deny a cosmic evil which affects our lives, Jesus very clearly states that sickness is not a by-product of any one person's sin. He says of the blind man, "It is not that this man or his parents sinned; he was born blind so that God's power might be displayed in curing him" (see John 9:1-3).

Nor does the Church look upon sickness, pain or death as punishment for one's personal sin. Granted, while sinful acts may make us tired and may cause us to feel pain, we can also get tired by praying too much. We can get the flu by visiting a sick neighbor; we can die trying to save someone else's life.

Jesus had no sin upon him, yet Jesus got tired, as when he crossed the lake to escape the crowds (see Mark 6:31-32). He had no sin upon him, yet he cried when Lazarus died (see John 11:35). He experienced his body just as we do: It got tired, it grieved, it ran tears, sweat and blood; it died.

We know Christ did not tolerate sickness. He treated it with much the same impatience as he did the money lenders in the Temple, the Pharisees, the faithless, or any other being or thing which would lead a little one astray. If we think about it, there is little that Jesus did not tolerate. He tolerated Judas's betrayal, the adulteress's sinful past, Peter's obstinacy and denial. He tolerated many things—except a refusal to believe in the word of God. Is sickness somehow like this—a refusal of God's order for our world? Is that why Christ saw it as something not to be tolerated but eliminated?

Why is it, then, when we pray for this elimination of a sickness, we seem unable to effect the cures he did? We want to say it is because we aren't God. Yet that really isn't the whole story, because Christ gave us his healing power. Perhaps the reason God does not effect healing through us is that we simply do not believe he will.

Instead of seeing a loving God, we see a God who punishes, a God of revenge. Humanity is sinful, we say. We brought it all upon ourselves in the Garden. Our ancestors sinned, and we have paid for it ever since. Worse, we believe our personal sinfulness caused our sickness in the first place.

But Peter, James and the early disciples were sinners, too. The New Testament makes quite a point of saying these followers were ordinary people. They became frightened, they had difficulty believing, they denied Christ, they drew swords, etc. They were no different from us. And just as their sinfulness did not cause their own sickness or prevent them from healing others, so our sinfulness is not the reason for our sicknesses and inability to heal.

We are all sinners. We will all be sick from time to time. Like all those whom Christ healed—even those he raised from death—we will all surely die. So it is not so much a lack of sinfulness (and according to this misguided reasoning, a lack of sickness) which we should strive for, but rather the acceptance of God's forgiveness. The former is the futility of human effort, the latter the mystery of Divine Love.

We should not dwell on sinfulness as much as focus on God's mercy. In the Gospels, it was never someone's sins that impeded a healing, for sins could be forgiven. It was the direction of their hearts which kept people from Christ. So, when praying for someone or for ourselves, we should examine our hearts. Is there hardness, bitterness? Are we angry toward our family, doctors, life, God himself? If so, we turn that over to Jesus' forgiveness and pray that he will remove any obstacle that is blocking our own faith in his using us as his instruments, that he work his healing in us and through us despite our own sinfulness.

St. Francis of Assisi was once a tortured soul who agonized over life and death, destruction and injustice. These issues plagued him, but they also drove him to change, to lay down his sword, take off his armor and serve in the army of the great, gentle King. In an age surrounded by merciless war and corruption in the Church, he did not harden his heart and turn from God, he clung to him. Francis didn't run from leprosy, he got down from his horse and embraced a leper. He didn't curse leprosy, nor did he curse God for letting it lay waste to human life.

In the book *Creative Suffering*, Alan Paton writes, "It is almost as though we said to God, 'Some say you are cruel, and we confess that the cruelty of the world troubles us, so that we have moments of doubt; but of your goodness, we have no doubt, having seen it in the life of Jesus. Therefore we put our lives in your hands, so that you may use them for the sake of others.' "

St. Francis, like many other saints, was chronically sick most of his life, so surely sanctity is not commensurate with longevity and good health. Sickness seemed to bring the saints closer to Jesus. We can't say they weren't healed because they lacked faith or were sinners. They weren't healed because their sickness helped them feel close to Christ; it did not harden their hearts, it strengthened them.

Faith, then, does not insure healing. It does enable

us to heal others, it helps us be healed; but it is not an essential element God needs before he can use his power. *We* need faith as an avenue to approach God; he can work with or without it.

An unanswered prayer, then, may not have anything to do with faith. It may simply be an expression of God's will. Perhaps then the greatest faith is to believe in the goodness and wisdom of his will, like Abraham, even when his will baffles our understanding and tears at our hearts. No one goes through life blithely, not even one who is close to God, not even Jesus who *is* God. Our humanity groans, St. Paul says, and when it does, we hurt.

Healing may or may not be a part of God's will for any one situation. But we must not let this blind us to the reality that it is God's very *nature* to heal. His presence is one of wholeness: wholeness of spirit, body and mind.

All the mental struggles I've mentioned in this book—attitude, adaptation, acceptance, self-doubt, anger, displacement, worthlessness—these things are just parts of who we are. I point them out as indications of steps and stages, things to look for and be aware of so that we can bring them to God—continuously bringing our self (good or bad, weak or strong) for him to fix, to build, to mold, to heal or not to heal, in whatever way he sees best.

We must never be fooled, however, into the temptation of thinking that we can do nothing but passively watch with folded hands and be as puppets to his play. St. Theresa of Avila says we must pray as if everything depended on God and work as if everything depended on us. Faith is not a magical thing that God simply responds to. It is like a partnership we can turn to, complain to, rest in, rely on. It is a dynamic life force between God and us, at times charged with heated words, at times warm and soothing, but never passive, never stagnant.

So, too, our approach to sickness should mirror such faith. Continuing in the words of Alan Paton, "There are many ways of reacting to it [suffering], but only one that is profitable, and that is to accept it, and use it and where possible, to prevent it, alleviate, bring it to an end."

14

Finding Meaning in Sickness

In coming to the close of this book, some of you may think, "What faith she must have to write such things!" Not true. Remember, I write now as one who is past the worst part of the storm. Were you to have asked me if I felt positive or optimistic in the middle of my sickness, I would have said, "No way!"

I hurt. And I never seemed to not hurt. It was very difficult to believe in myself, in any recuperative process, in the treatments afforded me. Had a considerable lessening of pain not occurred, I doubt that I would have written this book at all. And if it was hard to believe in human means, it was harder to believe in a benevolent God. So you see, though I paint a picture of hope, it is not because it is the easiest thing to paint, some gushing well of sweetness in my life, but rather because hope is the most elusive thing I have ever pursued. It needed to be caught and put on paper so that when I am without it, as I often am, I can reread what I have written and try to find it again.

To be honest, most of what I've said here makes me nervous—not because I don't think it is valid, but because I have taken such a brief look into human suffering. In that look, I sometimes cringe at my own inability to help, or even to heed my own words. My efforts to speak about spiritual truths I know are sometimes heard as platitudes or euphemisms. Human suffering is very, very real. Not to say thereby that spirituality is not, but to conclude that even Jesus, the ultimate Spirit, anguished in his mortal death.

I once heard a distinction between sickness and suffering. Sickness is something to conquer and overcome in order to show God's glory. Suffering, on the other hand, is something to expect as a by-product of Christian living. We will suffer persecution, misunderstanding, imprisonment, loss of family respect, etc. It is sickness we are to wipe out, not suffering.

But what words and distinctions can help when nothing seems to work? When our best efforts have failed? We *have* prayed. We *do* believe (at least we *did*). We sought all the human means possible, we have suffered greatly for our beliefs, yet we or someone we love still lie sick, dying.

In some ways I hate words because they aren't very comforting. They lie two-dimensional on the page when our soul cries out for three dimensional smiles, warmth, presence. We can't bury our heads in words when a husband or wife dies. Words have no hair to stroke, no scent to comfort us. If you are in any way like me, you may be more likely to slam the book closed and stick it back on the shelf or stuff it into a trash bag. Words can seem so useless without the manifestations they implore. In our very real grief, intellectualizing falls far short of the mark.

In *The Problem With Pain*, C.S. Lewis gave a logical, step-by-step explanation of human suffering. But 20 years later, when cancer consumed his wife, he himself found neither comfort nor reason in words. His pain led him to write yet another book, *A Grief Observed*. In it he pours out the angry feelings of a heart broken, a mind spent and a soul unable to understand. And so he writes, "But go to Him when your need is desperate, when all other help is in vain, and what do you find? A door slammed in your face, and a sound of bolting and double bolting on the inside. After that, silence. You may as well turn away. The longer you wait, the more emphatic the silence will become." And, "Not that I am (I think) in much danger of ceasing to believe in God. The real danger is of coming to believe such dreadful things about him. The conclusion I dread is not, 'So there's no God after all,' but 'So this is what God is really like. Deceive yourself no longer.' "

As a Christian, my experience with sickness could be likened to a rubber band. My faith was stretched to the limits. My understanding snapped, collapsed into an amorphous heap. I heard myself asking over and over, "If God is my Father and I am his child, why does he allow me to be sick? Does sickness come from God? If God is all-powerful, all-knowing and all-present, then he knows I am sick, where I hurt and that I need his power to make me well. Yet I remain sick."

In a human way it seems we have no other recourse but to believe that God is not out there. He does not hear. He does not give the privilege of Job's comfort to you and me. Our prayers seemingly fall silent and unheard. In the midst of health, it is so easy to believe—to be assured he cares, he lives and wants us to live, to be happy, to be alive. But in the throes of disease, pain or any manner of sickness and deprivation that threatens our life, it is difficult to believe he is a helping force. At times his power seemingly lies impotent.

Such dichotomy is not easily overcome. Yet I found that my human nature, complete with anger, tears, disillusionment, frustration, forgiveness and love, did more to bring me closer to a personal God than to keep me away. I think God yearns for our interaction with him. Why else would he invite us in Isaiah to, "Come now, let us argue it out"? If we look at the Bible as a whole, we do not see a history of people meekly accepting God's words and blissfully going to eternity. But rather we see the story of human nature. In a spiritual sense, our personal human struggle with God reflects all generations past and their struggles with God. My humanness makes it possible for me to approach God and others just as his humanness through Christ makes it possible for him to approach us, to approach me.

Sickness, then, at least has meaning. It enables us to see, if we will, all aspects of life. It aligns us with the mind of Christ and, like Christ, we long to free all of creation. To be truly Christlike, however, we must carry this knowledge into practice and on the day-by-day level use it to help others. We know pain. We know disease. We have felt it, seen it, smelled it; now we must act against it as Christ did.

It would seem then that the role of sickness in salvation might be as the impetus for transformation, the conversion of will: to take pain and bring as much wholeness from it as possible and to do that as Christ did, from the inside out; to understand humanity by becoming human; to bring salvation by carrying the marks of this world on one's body, to be the Mystical Body of Christ—one Body in many bodies, Christ in us as we are in Christ and we are in one another.

If sickness does play this role, then its part is one day ultimately to disappear. For then it will happen that creation has been freed and we have all died on our crosses, having spent ourselves on one another.

Afterword

When I first began to write this book, I felt I was staring into the depths of a black hole. What could I possibly say about pain and sickness that could help anyone else? As I struggled to fill this void, many people offered support, ideas, books, articles and stories that helped me find and create a way

So it is with life and all its vicissitudes. Alone we stare into black holes of space, pained and dying in our isolation. But in the decision to turn around and face the universe as it encompasses us—where we are, in our daily condition—we find countless other stars, in all directions of the darkness, twinkling.

For Further Reading

Augustine. *The Confessions of St. Augustine* (Garden City, NY: Image Books, 1960).

Cousins, Norman. *Anatomy of an Illness as Perceived by the Patient* (Boston: G.K. Hall, 1979).

Fox, Matthew. *Breakthrough: Meister Eckhart's Creation Spirituality in New Translation* (Garden City, NY: Doubleday, 1980).

Keller, Helen. *Midstream* (Garden City, NY: Doubleday, Doran and Co., 1929).

Kubler-Ross, Elisabeth. *On Death and Dying* (New York: Macmillan, 1969).

Lewis, C. S. *The Problem of Pain* (New York: Macmillan, 1962).

Lewis, C. S. *A Grief Observed* (New York: Seabury, 1961).

MacNutt, Francis. *Healing* (Notre Dame, IN: Ave Maria, 1974).

Menninger, Karl. *The Vital Balance* (New York: Viking, 1963).

Montagu, Ashley. *Touching: The Human Significance of the Skin* (New York: Columbia University, 1971).

Paton, Alan. *Creative Suffering: The Ripple of Hope* (Kansas City: Pilgrim Press and *The National Catholic Reporter,* 1976).

Rilke, Rainer Maria. *Selected Poems of Rainer Maria Rilke,* A Translation From the German and Commentary by Robert Bly (New York: Harper and Row, 1981).

Shlemon, Barbara. *Healing Prayer* (Notre Dame, IN:

Ave Maria, 1976).
Tournier, Paul. *Creative Suffering* (New York: Harper and Row, 1981).
White, Barbara Ehrlich. *Renoir, His Life, Arts and Letters* (New York: Harry N. Abrams, 1984).

Acknowledgments

Above everyone else, I would like to thank Murray for his patience, time, energy, love and support—not only in the writing of this book, but for all these years of standing by me in my sickness.

A special thanks to Dr. P. Prithvi Raj of the University of Texas Pain Control Center and to all the people of the University of Cincinnati Hospital Pain Control Center who made that place a warm and effective experience: Kathy, Kit, Doris, Jayne, Laurie, Mary Therese, Susan, Jenny, Elisheva and those whose faces I've said "hi" to but whose names I never knew.

To my old college roommates, Elaine, Diane and Cris, for taking care of me. Especially you, Diane, with those interminable ice packs.

I extend my love and gratitude to Alex and John whose care and emotional concern I could not have done without. Also to my friends Michael, Jeff, Joe, Deborah, Tom and Maureen.

And, lastly, a special wink to Al Silverglade who kept me on—even though I barely earned my keep.

*Also by Susan Saint Sing,
With Murray Bodo, O.F.M.*

**The Desert Speaks:
A Journey of Prayer for the Discouraged**

Popular audiocassette series of two tapes with music and narration. Say the authors: "These words are for everyone whose discouragement and pain have made life barren and hopeless. In words and song we have tried to enter this loneliness and travel with you through the heart's desert to the inner place where hope once again takes root in the soul."

Two cassettes in shelf-case, with lyrics. CAS 240 $15.95